DATE DUE

AVON PUBLIC LIBRARY
BOX 977 / 200 BENCHMARK RD.
AVON, COLORADO 81620

21.95 5/13 BJT

ANIMAL JOURNEYS

Migrating with the Caribou

Thessaly Catt

PowerKiDS
press

New York

Published in 2011 by The Rosen Publishing Group, Inc.
29 East 21st Street, New York, NY 10010

Copyright © 2011 by The Rosen Publishing Group, Inc.

All rights reserved. No part of this book may be reproduced in any form without permission in writing from the publisher, except by a reviewer.

First Edition

Editor: Amelie von Zumbusch
Book Design: Ashley Burrell

Photo Credits: Cover Jared Hobbs/Getty Images; p. 4 Panoramic Images/Getty Images; p. 5 (bottom) Photos.com/Thinkstock; p. 5 (top) Shutterstock.com; pp. 6, 22 iStockphoto/Thinkstock; p. 7 © www. iStockphoto.com/Mikadx; p. 8 © Juniors Bildarchiv/age fotostock; p. 9 Jerry Kobalenko/Getty Images; p. 10 (top) Tom Walker/Getty Images; pp. 10–11 © www.iStockphoto.com/Pierre Cardon; pp. 12, 15, 19 © Alaska Stock/age fotostock; p. 14 Peter Lilja/Getty Images; p. 16–17 Geoff Brightling/Getty Images; p. 18 © www.iStockphoto.com/Liz Leyden; pp. 20–21 Maria Stenzel/National Geographic/Getty Images.

Library of Congress Cataloging-in-Publication Data

Catt, Thessaly.
 Migrating with the caribou / by Thessaly Catt. — 1st ed.
     p. cm. — (Animal journeys)
 Includes index.
 ISBN 978-1-4488-2541-7 (library binding) — ISBN 978-1-4488-2666-7 (pbk.) — ISBN 978-1-4488-2667-4 (6-pack)
 1. Caribou—Migration—North America—Juvenile literature. 2. Caribou—North America—Juvenile literature. I. Title.
 QL737.U55C355 2011
 599.65'81568—dc22

                                        2010024146

Manufactured in the United States of America

CPSIA Compliance Information: Batch #WW11PK: For Further Information contact Rosen Publishing, New York, New York at 1-800-237-9932

Contents

The Caribou's Journey

Many animals stay close to the places they were born for their whole lives. Other animals, such as caribou, go on a long journey every year. This journey is called migration.

This caribou is making its spring migration through Alaska's Denali National Park.

Caribou live in Alaska, northern Canada, Scandinavia, and Russia. The caribou that live in Scandinavia and Russia are most often known as reindeer. Every spring, caribou migrate toward the places where they were born. They travel in big groups, called herds. The herds return to their winter

This herd of reindeer lives in Russia's Ural Mountains. Caribou and reindeer are really just two names for the same animal.

Since caribou live in cold places, they make part of their migration over snowy ground.

homes in the fall. Many herds travel hundreds of miles (km) in each direction. Caribou have been making this journey for thousands of years.

Caribou are part of the deer family. They stand between 3 and 5 feet (1–1.5 m) tall. Both male and female caribou have bony **antlers** on their heads.

The caribou lives farther north than any other member of the deer family. It gets very cold in the places where caribou

In the spring and summer, caribou antlers are covered in hairy skin, called velvet. In September, caribou shed the velvet, as this one is doing.

In the summer, caribou hooves grow soft. This makes it easier for caribou to walk over wet or rocky ground.

live. Caribou have shorter legs than other members of the deer family. Their short legs help them stay warm.

Caribou have **concave** hooves on their feet. They use their hooves to dig up snow when they are looking for food. They also have a good sense of smell that helps them find food under the snow.

Caribou in North America

This is a woodland caribou. Sadly, people have pushed woodland caribou out of many of the forests where they once lived.

In North America, there are three types of caribou. Peary caribou live on rocky islands in northern Canada. These caribou's light-colored coats help them blend in with the snow.

Woodland caribou live in Canada's **taiga**. Woodland caribou are the largest kind of caribou. They are always on the move in order to find food and keep safe from **predators**.

Barren-ground caribou are the most common kind of caribou. These caribou live in huge herds and make some of the longest migrations. They live in Alaska and in Canada's Yukon, Northwest, and Nunavut territories. The ones in Alaska are sometimes known as Grant's caribou.

These Peary caribou live on Axel Heiberg Island, in Nunavut, Canada. Since they live on islands, Peary caribou do not migrate as far as some other caribou do.

All About Migration

The place where a herd lives is called its range. Each year, caribou migrate between their summer and winter ranges. Summer ranges are often in the mountains or along the coast of the Arctic Ocean. In the summer, these places have

During their migration, caribou often have to swim across rivers. These caribou are crossing the Kobuk River, in Alaska.

plenty of food for caribou to eat. In the winter, though, they become very cold and snowy. The herds migrate to warmer homes in the fall.

In April, caribou start walking to their summer ranges. They cross hundreds of miles (km) of evergreen forests and **tundra**. By August, the caribou have started to fatten up. They are ready to begin their journey by September.

This herd of caribou is traveling across the tundra. Tundra has mainly low-growing plants, such as grass, moss, and wildflowers on it. The ground there is frozen for much of the year.

Caribou Migration

These migrating caribou are members of the porcupine herd. The herd has about 100,000 members. It is one of the most studied caribou herds.

Right: This map shows the range of the porcupine herd. In the summer, the herd stays near the places where the calves are born. In the winter, it travels inland.

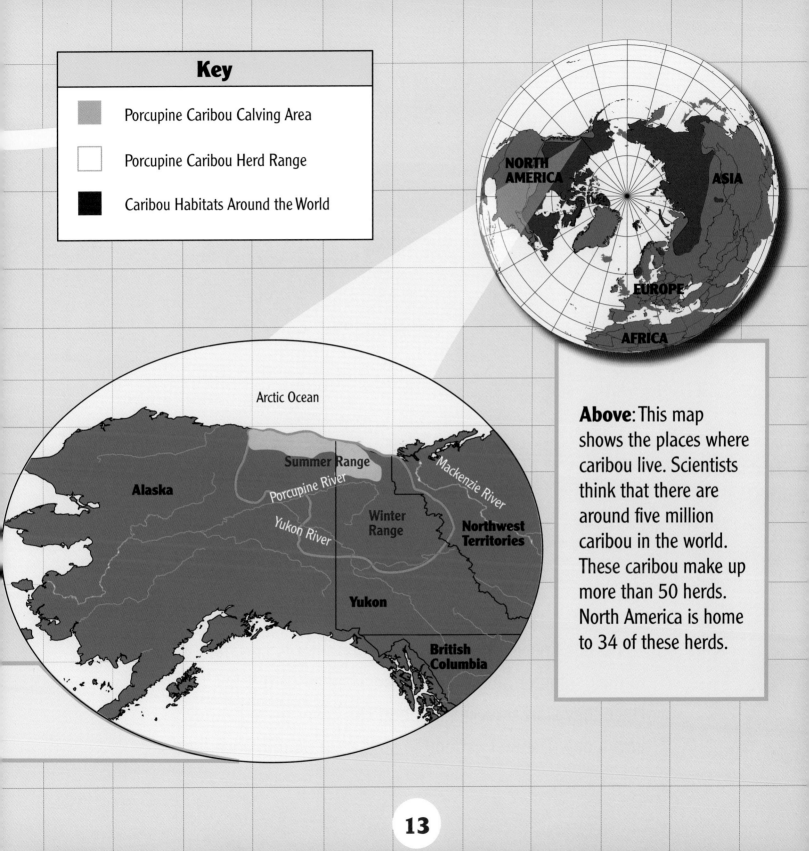

Key

- **Porcupine Caribou Calving Area**
- **Porcupine Caribou Herd Range**
- **Caribou Habitats Around the World**

NORTH AMERICA

ASIA

EUROPE

AFRICA

Arctic Ocean

Summer Range

Alaska

Porcupine River

Mackenzie River

Yukon River

Winter Range

Northwest Territories

Yukon

British Columbia

Above: This map shows the places where caribou live. Scientists think that there are around five million caribou in the world. These caribou make up more than 50 herds. North America is home to 34 of these herds.

Life in the Herd

Some caribou herds are very large. The biggest caribou herds have several hundred thousand members!

No one knows exactly how migrating herds find their ways to their summer ranges each year. They move quickly, though. Once they start traveling, caribou can cover up to 50 miles (80 km) a day. The first caribou to start migrating in each herd are the older females. The younger females and calves come next. A few weeks later, the male caribou follow.

In the fall, male caribou fight each other. This time is called the rut. The males crash their antlers together, trying to show that they are the strongest. Male caribou fight because they are trying to find **mates**.

When a male caribou wins a fight, he wins control of a piece of land. Males mate with the females that are on the land they control.

Caribou Calves

Each year, caribou herds return to the same calving grounds. These are special places where female caribou, called cows, give birth to caribou babies, called calves. The calves are born between May and July. When it is time for a cow to have her baby, she leaves the herd and finds a safe place to have the baby. The cow and calf rejoin the herd a few days later.

Caribou stay close to their mothers during their first few months. By fall, they have grown enough to look after themselves. Male caribou, called bulls, generally live for about 7 years. Female caribou can live for as long as 10 years.

Caribou cows most often give birth to just one calf each year. Sometimes, though, they have two babies at the same time.

Food and Predators

Caribou are **herbivores**. This means they eat only plants. Finding plants to eat is hard for migrating caribou since the ground is covered in snow for much of their journey. During spring and summer, caribou may eat Arctic cotton grass, willow

This caribou is eating lichen. Caribou eat several kinds of lichen. Reindeer lichen is one of the foods they eat most often.

Grizzly bears, such as these, are one of the kinds of bears that hunt caribou. Black bears hunt caribou, too.

leaves, mushrooms, or flower buds, depending on where they are. In the fall and winter, food is harder to find. During these seasons, caribou eat frozen **lichen**, dried **sedges**, or small shrubs.

Caribou have many natural predators. Wolves, wolverines, and bears are among the animals that hunt caribou. Golden eagles and lynx prey on caribou calves.

People hunt caribou, too. In fact, people have been hunting caribou for tens of thousands of years. In Alaska, hunters kill about 22,000 caribou for their meat each year. At times, hunters are not allowed to hunt caribou from certain herds if the **population** of that herd is getting too small. Caribou meat is an important food for the Inuits and other peoples who live in the Arctic parts of North America.

In Europe and Asia, people have raised **domesticated** reindeer for thousands of years. For example, the native peoples in Asia's Altai Mountains raise reindeer for their milk, meat, and skins.

These Nenets have gathered for a reindeer race. The Nenets are a people who live in northern Russia. They have a long history of raising reindeer.

The Future for Caribou

Today, people are destroying the places where caribou live. We cut down forests, build roads, and drill for oil in places through which caribou herds migrate.

Though there are many dangers facing caribou, people are trying to find ways to keep the world safe for these Arctic animals.

Climate change also causes trouble. It causes changes in weather that are a problem for caribou. Sometimes, caribou arrive at their summer ranges to find that the plants they generally eat have not yet grown or have already died.

Today, people are working to end climate change. We have also set aside some land for Arctic wildlife. With our help, caribou should be around for a long time.

Glossary

antlers (ANT-lerz) Large branchlike horns that grow on the heads of some animals.

climate change (KLY-mut CHAYNJ) Changes in Earth's weather that were caused by things people did.

concave (kon-KAYV) Dipping toward the center, like a spoon.

domesticated (duh-MES-tih-kayt-id) Raised to live with people.

herbivores (ER-buh-vorz) Animals that eat plants.

lichen (LY-ken) A living thing that is made of two kinds of living things, called an alga and a fungus.

mates (MAYTS) Partners for making babies.

population (pop-yoo-LAY-shun) A group of animals or people living in the same place.

predators (PREH-duh-terz) Animals that kill other animals for food.

sedges (SEJ-ez) Grasslike plants with solid stems that grow near water.

taiga (TY-guh) A forest with fir and spruce trees, or trees that have cones and needlelike leaves, which starts where a tundra ends.

tundra (TUN-druh) The icy land of the coldest parts of the world.

Index

A
Alaska, 5, 9, 20

C
Canada, 5, 8–9

F
fall, 5, 11, 15, 17, 19
feet, 7
food, 7–8, 10, 19–20

H
heads, 6
herbivores, 18

herd(s), 5, 9–11, 14,
    16, 20, 22
hooves, 7

L
lichen, 19

M
mates, 15
migration(s), 4, 9

P
population, 20
predators, 8, 19

R
reindeer, 5, 21
Russia, 5

S
Scandinavia, 5
sedges, 19
snow, 7–8, 18
spring, 5, 18

T
taiga, 8
tundra, 11
types, 8

Web Sites

Due to the changing nature of Internet links, PowerKids Press has developed an online list of Web sites related to the subject of this book. This site is updated regularly. Please use this link to access the list:
www.powerkidslinks.com/anjo/caribou/

AVON PUBLIC LIBRARY
BOX 977 / 200 BENCHMARK RD.
AVON, COLORADO 81620